curious about

CYCLOPS

BY GINA KAMMER

AMICUS LEARNING

What are you

curious about?

CHAPTER THREE

3

Finding Cyclopes

Curious About is published by
Amicus Learning, an imprint of Amicus
P.O. Box 227
Mankato, MN 56002
www.amicuspublishing.us

Editor: Ana Brauer
Series Designer: Kathleen Petelinsek
Book Designer: Kim Pfeffer
Photo Researchers: Katelynn Hope and Kim Pfeffer

Library of Congress Cataloging-in-Publication Data
Names: Kammer, Gina, author.
Title: Curious about cyclopes / by Gina Kammer.
Description: Mankato, MN : Amicus Learning, an imprint of Amicus, [2025] | Series: Curious about mythical creatures | Includes bibliographical references and index. | Audience: Ages 6–9 | Audience: Grades 2–3 | Summary: "Where did the cyclops come from? Learn about the Greek mythology surrounding Cyclopes in this question-and-answer book for elementary readers. Includes infographics, table of contents, glossary, books and websites for further research, and index"—Provided by publisher.
Identifiers: LCCN 2024017579 (print) | LCCN 2024017580 (ebook) | ISBN 9798892000956 (library binding) | ISBN 9798892001533 (paperback) | ISBN 9798892002110 (ebook)
Subjects: LCSH: Cyclopes (Greek mythology)—Miscellanea—Juvenile literature. Classification: LCC BL820.C83 K36 2025 (print) | LCC BL820.C83 (ebook) | DDC 398.21—dc23/eng/20240509
LC record available at https://lccn.loc.gov/2024017579
LC ebook record available at https://lccn.loc.gov/2024017580

Photo Credits: Adobe Stock/Alfi, 5; Alamy Stock Photo/ARTGEN, 18–19; Freepik/IT'S ORA, 15 (top left), Pikaso, 12–13; Getty Images/ZU_09, 14; Shutterstock/Anatoly Vartanov, 15 (bottom right), Daniel Eskridge, 7, Fer Gregory, 15 (top right), Grobler du Preez, 20, Michael Rosskothen, cover, Mirko Kuzmanovic, 10, NosorogUA, 15 (bottom left), Obsidian Fantasy Studio, 11; Wikimedia Commons/Berthold Werner, 20–21, Constantin Hansen, 8–9, Johann Heinrich Wilhelm Tischbein, 4, Josep Renalias, 17 (top)

Printed in China

CHAPTER ONE

What are Cyclopes?

In Greek, Cyclops means "round eye."

In Greek **myths**, Cyclopes were giants. At first, there were only three of them. Their names were Arges, Brontes, and Steropes. Their father was the sky god. Their mother was the Earth goddess. They were powerful creatures.

In some stories, Cyclopes are shepherds. They take care of sheep and goats.

What does a Cyclops look like?

It's scary! A Cyclops looks like a giant human. It's large and strong. But it only has one eye in the middle of its forehead. In ancient art, some have slits or marks where human eyes would be.

In stories, some Cyclopes are very ugly and have sharp teeth.

COMPARING SIZES
How big is a Cyclops?

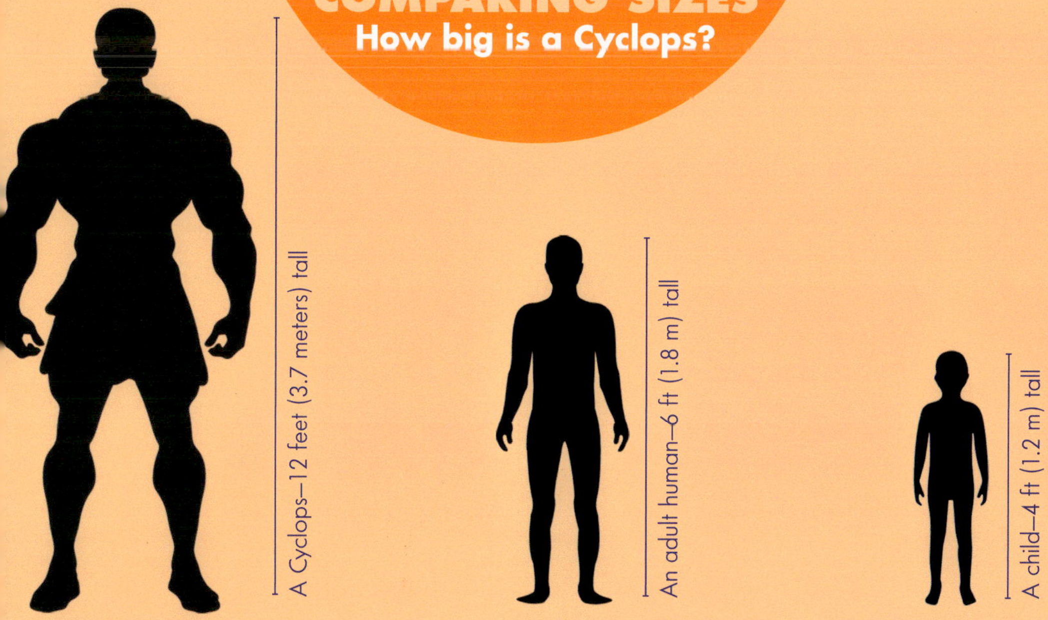

Are Cyclopes real?

In one story, a Greek hero and his men escaped a Cyclops by giving it wine until it fell asleep.

Not really! But stories about Cyclopes have been told for 2,000 years. In one myth, a man meets a Cyclops. It wants to eat him. He tricks it and escapes. Still, no one has hard **proof** they are real.

CHAPTER TWO

What does a Cyclops like to do?

A Cyclops is wild. But it works hard. A Cyclops can make thunder and lightning. In a **forge**, it shapes metal with a hammer. It makes weapons and armor. A Cyclops can build stone walls around cities. It even takes care of sheep!

In a forge, fire and hammers are used to shape metal into tools or weapons.

A Cyclops is very strong and can use very heavy weapons.

In stories, Cyclopes can live forever. But they often have short lives because they are killed.

How long does a Cyclops live?

Forever! But it's hard to know for sure. A Cyclops can be hurt or trapped. In one myth, Apollo kills the Cyclopes in revenge. Apollo is the Greek god of music and healing. A lightning bolt made by a Cyclops killed Apollo's son. The god was angry about the death of his son.

Are Cyclopes friendly?

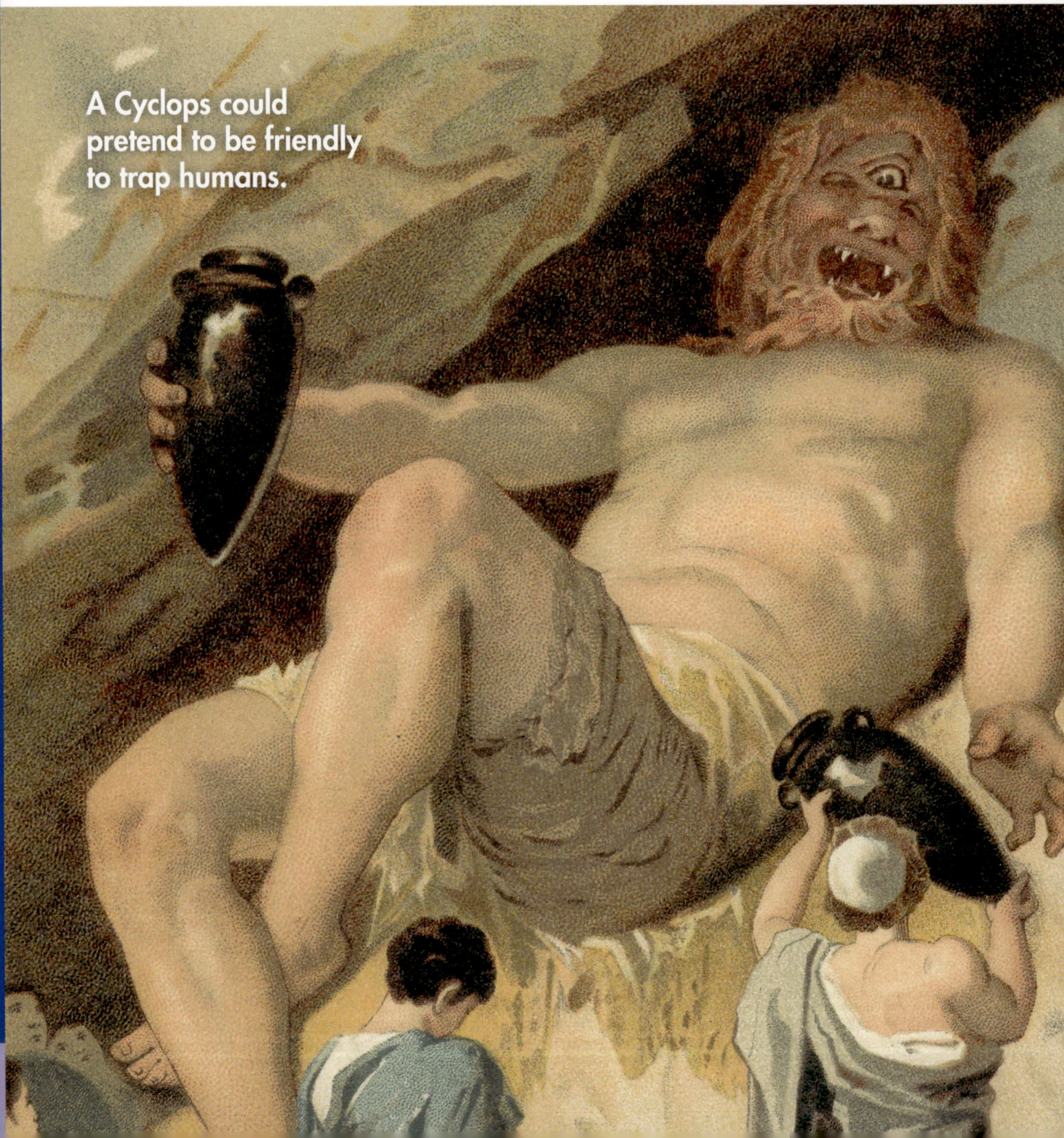

A Cyclops could pretend to be friendly to trap humans.

Probably not! Sometimes they eat people. So don't get on their bad side! You never know. They don't follow rules or laws. But Cyclopes did help Zeus, the king of the gods. They also made powerful weapons for the gods.

WEAPONS AND ARMOR MADE BY CYCLOPES

THUNDERBOLTS:
For Zeus, king of the gods and the sky

TRIDENT:
For Poseidon, god of the sea

BOW AND ARROWS:
For Artemis, goddess of hunting

HELMET OF INVISIBILITY:
For Hades, god of the dead and the underworld

Where do Cyclopes live?

Cyclopes live in faraway **wilderness**. In one story, they live in caves on an island. They might also live in volcanoes. That's where **legends** say they work for the gods. Cyclopes are said to **haunt** Mount Etna!

Mount Etna is an active volcano in Sicily, Italy. Some people think Cyclopes live there.

SITES TO SPOT CYCLOPES

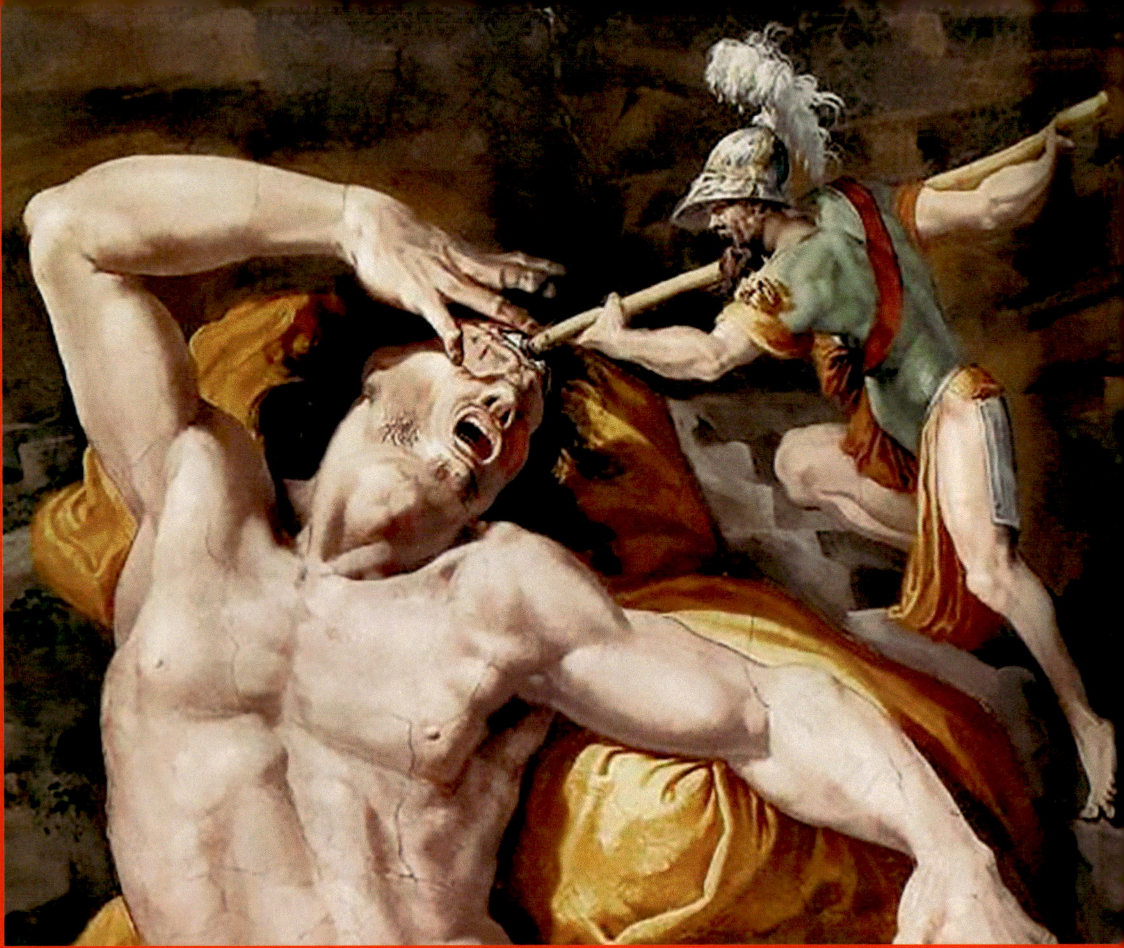

What hurts a Cyclops?

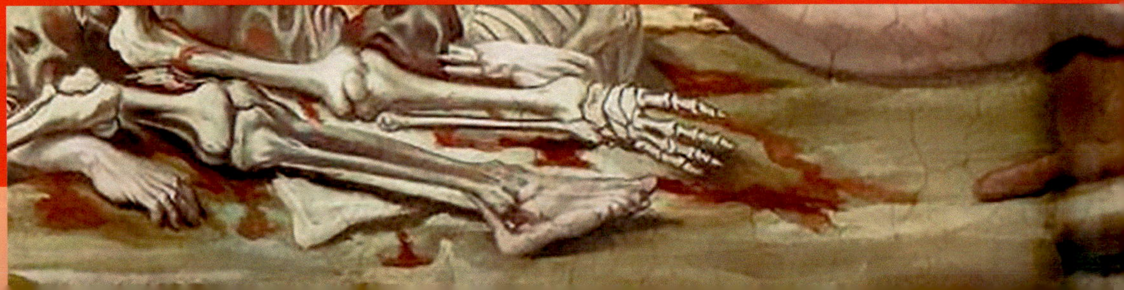

In most stories, the only way to beat a Cyclops is to blind it.

A poke in the eye! Or throwing it into Tartarus. That's a prison in the Greek underworld. But don't get into a fight with a Cyclops. It is strong. It attacks with fire and lightning. It can throw huge rocks. Watch out!

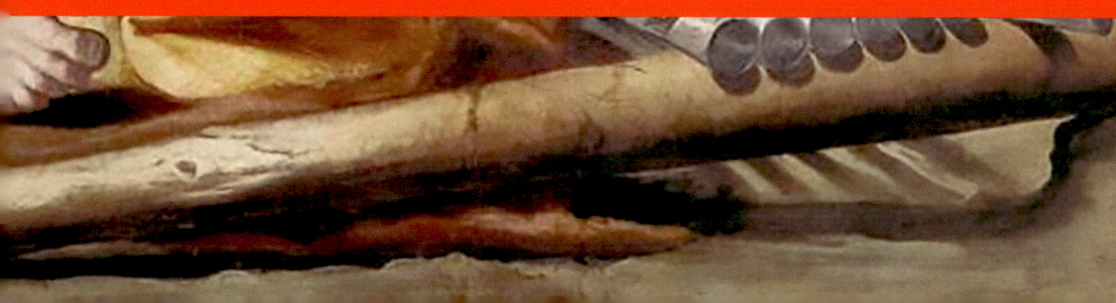

The skull of a dwarf elephant looks like it could belong to a Cyclops.

What else could the Cyclopes be?

A group of people who lived before the Ancient Greeks. Not giants! Just people who built walls with big rocks. The walls are called **Cyclopean** walls. Some still exist today. People likely thought these huge walls were built by giants.

Cyclopean walls are usually found in Greece and Italy.

STAY CURIOUS!

ASK MORE QUESTIONS

What stories have people told about Cyclopes?

Who were some famous Cyclopes in myths?

Try a BIG QUESTION: Why do people believe stories about giant creatures and gods?

SEARCH FOR ANSWERS

Search the library catalog or the Internet.
A librarian, teacher, or parent can help you.

Using Keywords
Find the looking glass.

Keywords are the most important words in your question.

If you want to know about:

- Cyclopes in Greek myths, type: CYCLOPS MYTHS
- Other Greek myths, type: GREEK MYTHOLOGY

LEARN MORE

FIND GOOD SOURCES

Are the sources reliable?
Some sources are better than others. An adult can help you. Here are some good, safe sources.

Books

Gaia: Goddess of Earth
by Imogen Greenberg, 2022.

Ultimate Greek Mythology: Adventurous Stories, Fun Facts, Amazing History, and Beyond!
L. J. Tracosas, 2023.

Internet Sites

Britannica Kids: Cyclops
https://kids.britannica.com/students/article/Cyclops/273888
Britannica is an encyclopedia with educational information on many topics.

National Geographic Kids: Gods and Goddesses of Ancient Greece
https://www.natgeokids.com/uk/discover/history/greece/greek-gods/
National Geographic has great information for curious kids.

Every effort has been made to ensure that these websites are appropriate for children. However, because of the nature of the Internet, it is impossible to guarantee that these sites will remain active indefinitely or that their contents will not be altered.

SHARE AND TAKE ACTION

Visit a museum of ancient history, or look one up online.
Find a piece of art, and write what you think it shows. Then read the museum's description, and compare.

Look up pictures of Cyclopean walls and other stone or brick walls.
With your family or friends, brainstorm how they might have been built.

Build your own stone wall.
Build a stone wall with small rocks, and imagine how hard it would be to build a large one.

GLOSSARY

Cyclopean A style of building with large stones set together with nothing between them.

forge A place where metal objects are made by heating and shaping metal.

haunt What a ghost does when it visits a place often.

legend A story from the past that may or may not be true but cannot be checked.

myth An idea or story that is believed by many people but that is not true.

proof Facts or evidence that show something is true.

wilderness A wild and natural area in which few people live.

INDEX

About the Author

Gina Kammer grew up writing and illustrating her own stories. Now she teaches others to write stories at inkybookwyrm.com. She likes reading fantasy and medieval literature. She also enjoys traveling, oil painting, archery, and snuggling her grumpy bunny. She lives in Minnesota.